Contents

Introduction

The sport of athletics began in the ancient Olympic Games about three thousand years ago. Since then more and more sports have been added. Athletics is now divided into two types, called track events and field events. Track events are running races. Field events involve throwing and jumping.

This book considers how under 13s participate in athletics. Unless otherwise stated, all the measurements, distances and weights mentioned in this book are for the under 13 age group.

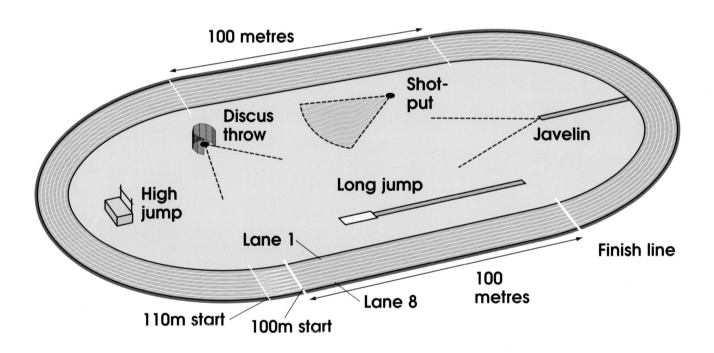

Most tracks are 400m in **circumference**. They are usually grass or made with a rubberized surface which gives a good grip for running. The field events take place on the grass area inside the track.

This table shows the main types of track and field events you are likely to compete in.

Track events	Field events
Short sprints	High jump
Medium-distance running	Long jump
Long-distance running	Javelin
Hurdles	Shot-put
Relay races	Discus

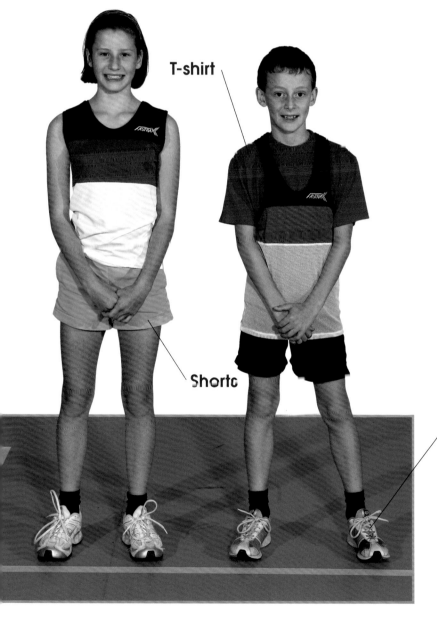

T-shirt

Shorts

Competitors' kit

Track and field events can be very energetic, so your clothing needs to be comfortable. Start off with loose shorts and a T-shirt, then perhaps add a tracksuit to warm up in and keep you warm between races or events.

Trainers

You need good trainers that support your feet. Spiked running shoes are available in small sizes for the really keen!

Warming-up drills

It is important to warm up properly before attempting running or jumping activities. First warm up your body with gentle jogging. Gradually increase your pace until you have been active for at least 10 minutes.

The high-knee walk

The high-knee walk involves walking with good **posture** and lifting your knees to be level with your hips. Make a right angle between your leg and your knee. Walk as tall as possible at all times.

Your elbow should make a right angle and your thumb should move from your hip to your mouth level (hip to lip) with each step.

The lunge walk

The lunge walk strengthens the leg muscles and is a warm up for sprinting. Take a large step forward, bending your back knee down to the ground. Repeat with the other leg.

Warm down

At the end of training you should keep moving and stretching while cooling down. This **hamstring** stretch (right) will stop your muscles tightening up after an active session.

Sprints

A sprint is a short running race of 50m, 60m, 100m, 110m, 150m or 200m. For the shorter distance sprints, you must try to run as fast as possible for the entire distance.

Starting a race

When the starter says 'On your marks', place one foot just behind the start line and the other a bit further back. Both legs should be slightly bent with the body weight over the front foot.

On the command 'Set', hold your body still and ready to push from your back foot. When the starter says 'Go', drive forward as fast as possible. Stay low and look straight down the track, gradually rising to an upright running position over the first five strides. All sprint races are run in lanes, and if you cross over into another lane you will be **disqualified**.

Running action

The leg movement for a sprinter should be quick and light. The arms should move with a smooth forward-backward action. The legs should drive forward with a high knee action and good stride length.

The finish

The sprint is a short race so there is no time for slowing down near the finish line. Athletes learn to thrust their chests out just before they cross the line.

Hurdles

A hurdling race is usually 70m long for girls and 75m for boys. There are eight **hurdles** which should be set so that you can fit three strides between each hurdle. As you clear the hurdle, push your front leg out straight ahead of you. The other leg follows, keeping the thigh, calf and foot parallel with the hurdle rail. Don't think so much about jumping the hurdle, rather 'sprint over it'.

Relays

During a relay race, members of a team take turns in running a length of the track, passing a **baton** to the next team member at each changeover of runner. A relay team consists of either four or eight runners and each runner covers a distance of 50 or 100m.

The upsweep

There are two ways of passing on the baton. In the upsweep (above) the receiving hand faces downwards with a wide angle between the thumb and the fingers.

The changeover

Each runner must hand over the baton to the next runner within a changeover zone, usually marked on the track. The second runner should start running before they have been handed the baton, but they mustn't pass beyond the end of the zone without it.

The downsweep

In the downsweep the receiving hand faces upwards. The incoming athlete passes the baton downwards into the receiving hand. This is not as easy to do as the upsweep, but it makes passing the baton on much quicker.

Endurance races

Races of over 800m are called **endurance** races. In these races, you start in separate lanes but can then break away and move across the track to the inside (shortest) lane.

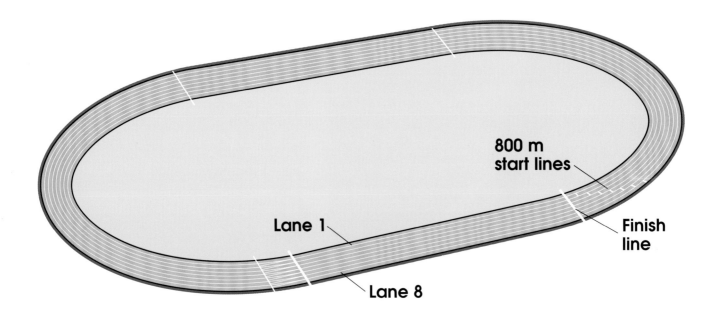

800 m start lines

Finish line

Lane 1

Lane 8

Running technique for endurance races

Running longer distances involves learning how to run well in a group, and how to avoid getting blocked by other runners. You should run with a much lower knee lift and a more relaxed arm action. The idea is to conserve as much energy as possible.

One of the first things you have to learn is pace judgement – learning how to run at a speed which you can keep up for the whole race. If you start off too quickly you will be overtaken by people with better pace judgement.

Cross-country running

Many schools do cross-country running as a form of endurance running. A cross-country race will cover between 1,000m and 3,000m.

Cross-country running is very different to running on a track. The ground may be hilly, uneven or slippery. Spiked running shoes will be needed. You will use a shorter stride length to give you more control, but greater leg speed. You will have to make constant adjustments in balance and use more muscles. A cross-country runner does not need to run at the same speed as a sprinter, but needs good powers of endurance.

The marathon

The longest distance running event in the Olympic Games is the marathon. The marathon has an official distance of 42.195 kilometres (26 miles 385 yards) and is considered the ultimate test of **stamina** and determination. The women's record is held by Paula Radcliffe (left) of the United Kingdom. It was set during the 2005 London Marathon, with an official time of 2 hours 17 minutes and 42 seconds.

High jump

The high jump is a field event in which competitors must jump over a **horizontal** bar. The bar is moved up to higher levels until the competitor can no longer clear it.

High jump run-up

The run-up to the jump consists of eight strides; three in a straight line and five round the curve. The body should **accelerate** and lean in the direction of the curve. The take-off should be from the left foot.

8 7 6 5 4 3 2 1

The scissors jump

This is the safest type of jump as it allows the jumper to land on their feet. The leg nearest the bar should be swung into the air to clear the bar. As you cross the bar, the trailing leg must be swung quickly up to clear the bar. While this is happening the first leg should be driven downwards. This up and down movement of the legs is similar to the action of scissors.

The Fosbury Flop

The Fosbury Flop jump should only be tried with the help of a qualified coach and requires a deep foam mat to catch you. The jump is backwards over the bar and the landing is on the back and shoulders.

Dick Fosbury

The Fosbury Flop got its name from an American high jumper called Dick Fosbury. He caused a sensation in the 1968 Olympic Games by jumping over the bar backwards! He won a gold medal for his jump and now the Fosbury Flop is a popular style of high jump for most Olympic jumpers.

Long jump

The long jump is an event where athletes attempt to jump as far as possible from their take-off point. The simplest way to understand the long jump is to think: 'Run as fast as you can and jump as high as you can!'

1. The approach run

You need to be able to run really fast to make a good jump. Young long jumpers should take as many strides as their age, so if you are 12, take 12 strides.

2. The take-off

Hitting the board correctly is very important. It must be as fast as possible with a short final stride. Jump up, but try not to sacrifice speed for height.

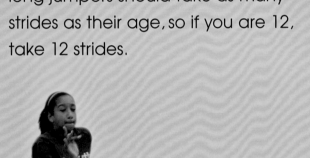

Foul line

Competitors run down a track and jump from a take-off board, usually called the 'board'. The edge of the board is called the foul line. Your foot should be as close as possible to the foul line but not go over it. It is marked with a line of Plasticine which will be dented if the foot touches it.

3. Action in the air

Bring your arms behind your body and above your head to help keep your body upright.

4. The landing

Aim to get your heels as far away from the board as possible.

Do not allow yourself to fall backwards on landing. The distance measured as your jump is the nearest mark made in the sand from the board.

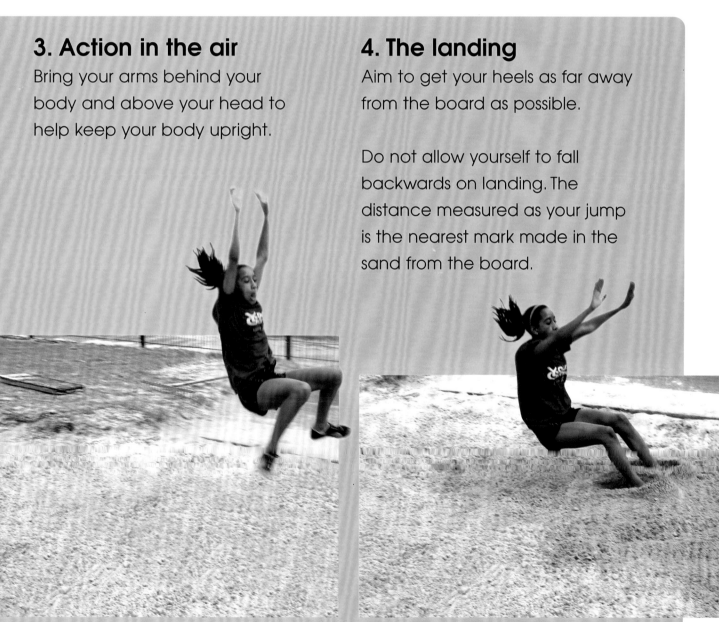

Shot and discus

The shot or shot-put event involves throwing or 'putting' a heavy metal ball (the shot) as far as possible. The competitors take their throw from inside a circle measuring 2.14m in diameter. The shot weighs 2.72kg for girls and 3.25kg for boys.

Putting

The thrower must rest the shot close to their neck and keep it close while throwing. At the end of the throw, the thrower must push the ball off the fingertips – not throw it. The shot must land within two white lines radiating from the edge of the throwing circle. The distance thrown is measured from where the shot first touches the ground to the edge of the circle. Each competitor has a certain number of throws, usually three or four.
The winner is the person with the furthest put.

Throwing area

Throwing circle

Discus

The discus event is similar to the shot-put except that it involves throwing a heavy disc. The discus weighs 0.75kg for girls and 1kg for boys. A full size adult discus is usually made of wood and metal, however younger athletes are more likely to use a solid rubber one which is easier to throw. The throw is taken from within a 2.5m circle.

The thrower usually starts off by doing a standing throw but later may be taught to spin in order to build momentum before releasing the throw. The launch must be smooth – if the discus wobbles it won't fly as far. The discus must land within an arc marked by lines on the landing zone. The throw is measured to where the discus first touches the ground.

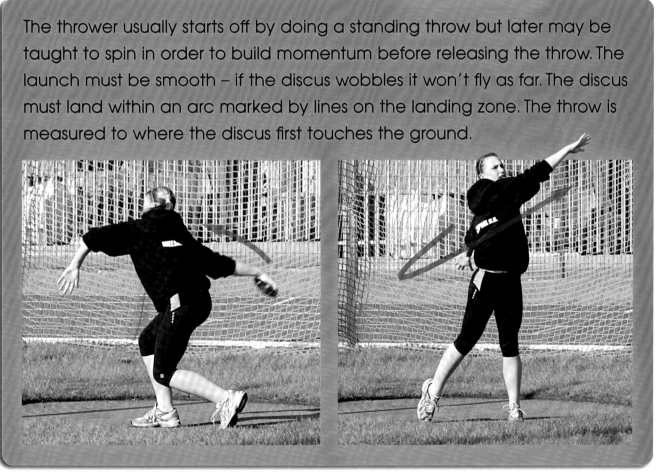

Javelin

The javelin event is a spear-throwing contest that began in ancient Greece as a part of the training of soldiers.

The javelin is a lightweight spear made of metal, **fibreglass** or **carbon fibre**. The javelin weight is 400g for both girls and boys. Throwers run down a track and throw the javelin before they reach a line.

Throwing technique

There are several different ways to hold a javelin, but most athletes use the 'Finnish' method.

To do this you grip the javelin between your thumb and your last three fingers, with your index finger underneath it.

First, practise throwing the javelin from standing. Then add a short run-up. This will lengthen with experience. The javelin should be carried behind you at shoulder height and almost parallel with the ground.

Just before you reach the line, the throwing arm moves further back and the javelin is pointed at a 45° angle upwards. As you take your last step, your hips should be pushed forward and the arm brought through 'fast and last'. The javelin should be thrown over the top of the head.

The javelin must land within the fan-shaped landing area at the end of the run-up. It must land point first. The length of the throw is measured from the line to where the javelin point first touches the ground.

Sports hall athletics

Track and field athletics always used to be an outdoor sport which took place during the summer months. However now many schools have sports halls that enable these activities to be carried on all through the year. Indoor athletics needs some adaptations, but many people find they can learn techniques and maintain their fitness all year round.

Track events

Competitors run in straight lines along the length of the hall, starting and finishing in the middle, and making turns at each end with the help of **reversaboards** (below).

As you approach the reversaboard, your speed should drop. You place your leading foot on the board's surface. You should aim to strike the middle or below the centre of the board to maintain good balance through the turn.

Standing long jump

The standing long jump is a two footed jump done from a standing position over a **graduated** landing mat. Bend your knees and swing your arms for lift. The length of the jump is measured from the take-off line to the back of the closest heel on landing. You may step forward after the jump, but any movement backwards is a no jump.

Soft javelin throw

The **soft javelin** is thrown from a standing position, with both feet behind the throwing line. The throw is measured from the throwing line to where the tip of the javelin first hits the ground.

Clubs and competitions

There are many reasons to get involved with athletics. The varied running, jumping and throwing activities will keep you fit and healthy.

Being an athlete can be a very rewarding hobby. It is fun to be part of a team and travel to different places to enter competitions. You will make new friends and achieve new personal goals.

If you do well, you can represent your school, county or even your country at the Olympic Games!

Olympic Winner

This picture shows Christine Ohuruogu of Great Britain winning the Women's 400m Final and the gold medal at the 2008 Olympic Games in Beijing, China.

The best way to get started in athletics is to join a local club. Here fully-qualified instructors will introduce you to the field events, javelin, shot, discus and long and high jump, and coach you in the different running techniques. By trying out all the different events you can find out which one you are best at.

You can find out where your nearest local club is by checking out the websites on page 29.

Glossary

accelerate to go faster

baton a short stick

carbon fibre very long, thin strands of carbon that are woven together to make a light but strong material

circumference the distance around something

disqualified removed from a competition

endurance the ability to last a long time

fibreglass a lightweight material made of woven glass fibres

graduated marked out in regular measurements

hamstring the group of muscles in the back of your thigh

horizontal flat and level with the ground

hurdles a frame that you run over in a race

posture the way in which you hold your body

reversaboard a board that helps you change direction in indoor races

soft javelin a beginner's javelin made of foam and rubber

stamina the energy needed to do something for a long time

Further reading

Field Athletics: Know Your Sport, Rita Storey,
Franklin Watts, 2008

Track Athletics: Know Your Sport, Chris Oxlade,
Franklin Watts Ltd, 2006

Track Athletics: Clever Clogs: the Olympic Sports, Jason Page,
Ticktock Media Ltd, 2008

Field Athletics: Clever Clogs: the Olympic Sports, Jason Page,
Ticktock Media Ltd, 2008

Track Athletics: Training to Succeed, Rita Storey,
Franklin Watts, 2009

Further information

UK Athletics
Athletics House
Central Boulevard
Blythe Valley Park
Solihull
West Midlands
B90 8AJ
Website: www.ukathletics.net

Youth Athletics in the UK
Website: www.boja.org

Indoor Sportshall Athletics
Sportshall Associates Limited
Unit 11, Wincham Avenue
Wincham
Northwich
Cheshire
CW9 6GB
Website: www.sportshall.org

Athletics Australia
Suite 22 Fawkner Towers
431 St Kilda Road
Melbourne
Vic 3004
Website: www.athletics.com.au

Index